Killer Bees

by Marcia Hinds

CAPSTONE BOOKS

an imprint of Capstone Press
Mankato, Minnesota

Capstone Books are published by Capstone Press
151 Good Counsel Drive, P.O. Box 669, Mankato, Minnesota 56002
http://www.capstone-press.com

Library of Congress Cataloging-in-Publication Data
Hinds, Marcia, 1955–
    Killer bees/by Marcia Hinds.
    p. cm.—(Dangerous animals)
    Includes bibliographical references and index.
    Summary: Details the characteristics, habitat, and life cycle of the Africanized honeybee, sometimes referred to as the killer bee.
    ISBN 1-56065-618-2
    1. Africanized honeybee—Juvenile literature. [1. Africanized honeybee. 2. Bees.] I. Title. II. Series.
QL568.A6H48 1998
595.79'9—dc21   97-8319
                                                                                       CIP
                                                                                       AC

Photo Credits
Victor Englebert, 6, 8, 11, 16, 21, 22, 26, 31, 32, 34, 36, 41
USDA Information Department, cover, 4, 5, 12, 15, 18, 24, 38, 42-43

The author wishes to thank Dr. Marla Spivak, Dr. Shimanuki, and Meg Mannix for their assistance with this project.

Capstone Books thanks Kim Kaplan of the U. S. Department of Agriculture for her assistance in preparing this book.

2 3 4 5 05 04 03 02 01 00

Table of Contents

Killer Bees

1) Are slightly smaller than European honeybees. Only an expert can tell the bees apart.
2) Have stripes.
3) Have hair all over their bodies.
4) Females can only sting once. Then they die.
5) Cannot live through cold winters. Found only in warmer areas.
6) Eat nectar and pollen and make honey.
7) Do dances to tell other bees how to find food.
8) Originally came from Africa.
9) Are quick to attack in defense of their hives.
10) May attack in great numbers.
11) Are not selective about where they build hives.
12) Swarm often.
13) Are easily upset.

European Honeybees

1) Are about one inch (two and one-half centimeters) long.
2) Have stripes.
3) Have hair all over their bodies.
4) Females can only sting once. Then they die.
5) Can live through cold winters.
6) Eat nectar and pollen and make honey.
7) Do dances to tell other bees how to find food.
8) Originally came from Europe.
9) Are less likely to defend their hives.
10) Usually do not attack in great numbers.
11) Are selective about where they build hives.
12) Do not swarm often.
13) Are calm and mild-mannered.

Chapter One

The Killer Bee

Bees born from mating European honeybees with African honeybees are called Africanized honeybees. A honeybee is a bee that makes honey from nectar. Nectar is a sugary liquid made in plants. Many people call Africanized honeybees killer bees because the bees have attacked and killed people.

A killer bee looks like an ordinary honeybee that people often see on flowers. But a killer bee's appearance can fool people. A killer bee is different in some dangerous ways.

Behavior

Behavior is the biggest difference between killer bees and other honeybees. Killer bees react more quickly than other honeybees. When killer bees

Killer bees react more quickly than other honeybees.

More than 50,000 killer bees can be involved in an attack.

feel danger, they rush out to defend their hive. They attack in greater numbers than other honeybees. Sometimes more than 50,000 killer bees will be involved in an attack.

A killer bee is also more aggressive. Aggressive means fierce. Each killer bee will sting when it is angry. Victims may get stung hundreds of times each minute because so many killer bees attack.

Other honeybees only attack if people are very close to their hives. But killer bees attack if they sense movement within 50 feet (15 meters) of their hives. The sound or movement of lawnmowers and other machinery has made killer bees attack, too.

Killer bees sometimes chase their victims more than one-half mile (about one kilometer). They stay angry for days after being disturbed.

Killer bee attacks are very frightening and dangerous. But too many people think only

---

Killer Bee Attack—
Costa Rica, July 1986

Inn Saing Ooi was a 24-year-old college student from the University ˈ Miami. One day he and some friends were exploring caves in Costa ica. Ooi was alone by the cave when he accidentally upset a killer e nest. His friends heard him scream. They saw him swinging his ms at the thousands of bees that surrounded him. In minutes, Ooi's dy was covered with angry, stinging killer bees.

His friends tried to rescue him, but the attacking killer bees forced em away. Two of his friends were hospitalized. One of them had ore than one hundred stings. The killer bees stayed angry. They ould not let anyone near Ooi until after dark. Ooi was later found ad. His foot had become stuck between two rocks and he could not n from the killer bees. He had been stung more than 8,000 times.

about the bee attacks. They do not realize that killer bee attacks are unusual. More people are killed by lightning than by killer bees. Every year, about 100 people die from lightning strikes. But in the past 40 years, only about 60 people have died as a result of killer bee attacks.

Scientists who study insects are called entomologists. Entomologists believe that killer bees are misunderstood. They do not feel the bees deserve the name killer.

The Spread of Killer Bees

Scientists brought African bees to Brazil in 1956. Scientists were trying to develop bees that would produce more honey in warmer climates. Someone released the bees into the wild. No one knows who released the bees.

The African bees were very aggressive. These aggressive bees mated with the mild-mannered local honeybees. The local honeybees were brought over from Europe in the

Scientists who study insects are called entomologists.

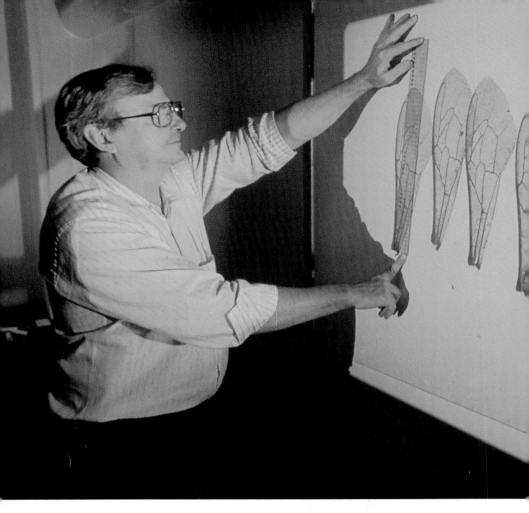

Entomologists measure the body parts of bees.

1800s. The bees born from mixing African bees with European bees behaved like the aggressive African bees. These bees became known as Africanized honeybees or killer bees.

Some killer bees took over the European bee hives. Over time, killer bees replaced the European bees.

Soon killer bees began spreading into other areas. They are now the most common type of bee in Central America and South America. Killer bees entered the United States near Hidalgo, Texas, in 1990. Since then, they have spread into other warm parts of the United States. There are now billions of killer bees in South America and North America.

Appearance

Killer bees and European honeybees look a great deal alike. Killer bees are a little darker. Killer bees also weigh less than other honeybees. Some killer bee body parts are smaller, too.

Still, entomologists cannot recognize killer bees by just looking at them. They have to use microscopes to examine the bees. Entomologists measure 25 different body parts to determine if a honeybee is European or Africanized.

Every honeybee has a similar body structure. Its body has three main parts. The front part is the head. The head is shaped like a triangle and is the smallest part of the body. A honeybee's head houses its large eyes, mouth, and antennas. An antenna is the feeler on an insect's head.

The middle part of a honeybee's body is the thorax. A bee's wings and six legs are attached to the thorax.

The rear part of a honeybee's body is the abdomen. A killer bee's abdomen is reddish-brown with black bands. Every female bee has a stinger. A stinger attaches to the end of the abdomen. A male bee does not have a stinger.

A honeybee's entire body is covered with hair. Even its eyeballs have hair on them. Hair helps a honeybee collect the pollen it eats as food. Pollen is a tiny yellow grain made in flowers. Pollen sticks to a honeybee's hair.

Pheromones

Killer bees react more quickly than European honeybees. This is because they are more sensitive to pheromones. Pheromones are

Killer bees use their hairs to collect pollen from plants.

chemicals. All honeybees communicate by releasing pheromones. Pheromones help bees identify each other. They also tell bees where to nest and where to find food.

The alarm pheromone tells bees to attack because their hives are in danger. The alarm pheromone that signals a stinging attack smells like bananas. Killer bees react more strongly to the alarm pheromone than other kinds of honeybees do.

What to Do When Stung

1) Remove the stinger quickly by taking an object with a hard edge and scraping the stinger out with a sideways motion.
2) Do not let the stinger stay in the skin. It will continue to release more venom into a victim's body for 10 minutes.
3) Do not pinch the stinger when taking it out. Pinching it will release more venom.
4) Do not cut the skin or try to suck out the venom. This could make the wound worse.
5) Putting ice on the sting can help reduce swelling. Putting a medicine cream on the sting might reduce pain.
6) People with allergies should go to the hospital right away. People without allergies should see the doctor if the sting does not heal.

Pheromones help bees identify each other.

Chapter Two

Life in the Colony

Killer bees live together in groups called colonies. Colonies may include up to 60,000 bees. Each colony lives in a hive.

Every bee has its own job to do. All the bees work together to keep their colony functioning smoothly. Queens, drones, and workers are the three types of bees found in each colony.

Killer Bee Queens

The queen is one type of female bee. A queen is larger than the other killer bees in the colony. There is only one queen in each colony.

Many queens hatch from eggs, but only one queen can rule. A new queen must either fight the ruling queen for control or leave the colony.

Queens are larger than other bees in the colony.

If the ruling queen is old or weak, a new queen fights to take over the colony. This new queen kills any eggs that are growing into queens. That way the new queen remains the only ruler.

Every queen has a stinger that can sting over and over again. But the stinger is used only to battle other queens. These battles decide who will rule the colony.

The queen's main job is to lay eggs. She also controls the behavior of the other killer bees by releasing pheromones. A queen is the only female in the hive that can lay eggs. A queen releases a pheromone called queen substance. Queen substance keeps the rest of the female bees from laying eggs.

Killer Bee Drones

A drone is a male killer bee. Its only job is to mate with a queen from another colony. A drone cannot mate with the queen from its own colony. It must leave its colony to find a mate. A drone

A drone's job is to mate with a queen.

does not have a stinger. This is because he does not protect the hive.

Drones die after they mate. Drones who do not find a queen to mate with die, too. The other bees force the drones out of the hive in the fall. The drones eventually starve. Starve means to suffer or die from lack of food.

Killer Bee Workers

Worker bees are females. They are responsible for all the work in the colony. Each worker performs a different job.

Some worker bees care for the queen. They clean and feed her. They also protect her.

Other worker bees gather food. They fly outside the hive to find a food source. After these bees find food, they come back to the colony. They perform a dance that tells other worker bees where the food is.

Some worker bees make honeycombs. A honeycomb is a wax structure that contains many hexagon-shaped cells. A hexagon is a

Worker bees do all the work in the colony.

six-sided shape. These workers use their wax to build the honeycomb. Bees store pollen, honey, and eggs in the cells.

Some of the workers are guard bees. These bees protect the killer bee colony. Guard bees know which bees belong to the colony. They know because each member of the colony carries the same scent.

Guard bees check the identity of all bees that enter the hive. Guard bees attack bees that do not carry the colony's scent. Killer bee colonies have more guard bees than other honeybee colonies.

Some workers are scout bees. Scout bees find places for new hives. They release another kind of pheromone that smells like lemons. This pheromone helps guide the bees to the new hive's location.

Other worker bees do many jobs. They help care for the eggs and defend the hive. They also help clean waste and dead bees from the honeycomb cells.

Some workers keep honeycomb cells clean.

Chapter Three

Survival

Killer bee populations spread quickly because they swarm more often than other honeybees. Swarming is when part of a colony leaves to form a new colony. Killer bees swarm when their hive has become too crowded.

Swarming

Sometimes part of the colony swarms when a new queen hatches. The older queen swarms with part of the colony. The newly hatched queen rules over the colony members that stay behind.

More than one swarm can arise from a single colony. Another new queen may hatch and fly off with part of the remaining colony.

Killer bees swarm more often than other honeybees.

Where the Killer Bees Live

No one knows why some bees swarm and other bees remain behind.

Bees stuff themselves with honey before swarming. This gives them the energy they need to fly to a new location. Killer bees can travel more than 100 miles (160 kilometers) to

28

look for a new home. Other honeybees cannot swarm for such long distances.

New killer bee colonies can produce another swarm in only 50 days. Other honeybees take longer to swarm. Killer bees are spreading into new areas at a rate of 300 miles (480 kilometers) a year.

Mating

Newly born queens cannot lay eggs until they mate. But they cannot mate with drones from their own colonies. They must attract drones from other colonies.

The new queens leave their colonies. As they fly, they release pheromones that attract drones. The drones chase the queens in a high-speed flight. They may be up to 100 feet (30 meters) in the air. The bees mate during the flight.

Queens mate with eight to 12 different drones during the mating flight. This gives the queens the ability to lay eggs throughout their lives. Queens never mate again. They return to their colonies and begin laying eggs.

Eggs

Queen killer bees can lay 3,000 to 6,000 eggs a day. This is almost twice as many eggs as European honeybee queens can lay. This is another reason that killer bees spread faster than other honeybees.

Queens lay eggs in honeycomb cells. Worker bees take care of the eggs. They feed several of the eggs royal jelly for about 15 days to hatch a queen. Royal jelly is a special food made up of chemicals released from a bee's body. Sometimes royal jelly is called bee milk.

Bees feed the young bees royal jelly for three days if they want to hatch workers. Bees feed the young bees pollen and honey after the three days.

As adults, both queens and workers eat nectar and pollen.

Absconding

Sometimes bees run out of food. European honeybees will starve rather than leave the hive. Killer bees will abscond instead. Abscond means to leave suddenly.

Killer bee queens can lay 3,000 to 6,000 eggs a day.

Killer bees inject venom into victims when they sting.

Killer bees will find another place to live or will die trying. Because they do not stay in their hives, they are more difficult for beekeepers to manage. This also limits the amount of honey they produce.

During winter, European honeybees stay in their hives to keep warm. They eat the honey they made during the summer. Killer bees do not store much honey. They swarm too often. Without a lot of honey, killer bees cannot live through winter. This is why killer bees prefer warm climates.

Stings

Guard bees and other worker bees have stingers. They use their stingers to attack anything that seems to put their hive in danger. Killer bees attack quickly and without warning. They attack as a group. A group of killer bees can sting people hundreds of times in a matter of minutes.

Unlike a queen, each worker bee can only sting once. Their stings inject venom into their victims. Venom is liquid poison produced by some animals. But killer bee venom is no more poisonous than venom from other bees. Killer bees are dangerous because so many bees may sting a victim at once.

A bee's stinger has barbs on it. A barb is a hook. The barbs anchor the stinger into the skin of

Killer Bee Attack— Brazil, May 1965

A man tried to burn a killer bee nest that was in his chimney. Within three hours, the bees had stung 500 people. One man had so many stingers in his bald head that he said that he thought he was growing hair again.

The bees attacked animals at nearby farms. They left behind dead chickens and hurt 12 dogs. They also stung two horses so many times that the horses could not eat for three days.

the victim. A killer bee flies away after it stings. But its stinger rips out of the bee's body and stays attached to the victim. The stinger continues to release venom into the victim until it is removed. The bee bleeds to death without its stinger.

Surviving Killer Bee Attacks

One bee sting can kill a person who has an allergic reaction. An allergic reaction is a sickness or skin problem caused by contact with a chemical. Only one person out of every 100 has an allergy to bee stings.

A person without allergies can survive 10 bee stings for every pound he or she weighs. That means someone weighing 200 pounds could be stung 2,000 times and still survive. One person attacked by killer bees was stung 2,243 times and still lived. A child weighing 50 to 60 pounds (22 and one-half to 27 kilograms) can survive 500 to 600 stings.

Only one person out of 100 has an allergy to bee venom.

Some people who come in contact with killer bees do not get stung. The killer bees in this pole did not attack.

Killer bees are most dangerous to older people who cannot run away. Young people who do not know what to do are also in danger. Even so, the average person can outrun any type of bee if it is attacking.

It is true that killer bees sometimes attack in large numbers. But it is still rare for killer bee attacks to involve large numbers of bees. Some people who come into contact with killer bees

leave without being stung. Other people are stung just a few times.

Surviving a Killer Bee Attack

Here are some things people should do if attacked by killer bees:

1) Run in a zigzag pattern away from the killer bees.
2) Protect the face by shielding it with the arms.
3) Try to get inside a building or a car as quickly as possible.
4) Do not jump into water. The killer bees will wait above the water. The bees will sting when you surface for air.
5) Do not swat or crush bees. Crushed bees release a smell that makes other bees attack in greater numbers.

Chapter Four

Killer Bees and People

Killer bees are honeybees. Honeybees are among the most useful types of insects. Plants would not be able to produce seeds or grow fruits and flowers without honeybees. Many kinds of plants would die without honeybees. Then people would not be able to eat the food the plants produce.

Pollination

Bees collect pollen. Plants need pollen from other plants to reproduce. Bees store the pollen they collect on short, stiff hairs on their back legs.

Killler bees collect pollen.

These hairs are called pollen baskets. The bees take pollen back to their hives. They store pollen in honeycomb cells and eat it as food.

Grains of pollen stick to their hairs as bees fly from flower to flower. Some of the pollen grains rub off when bees fly to other flowers. This process is called pollination. A plant uses the pollen from another plant to produce its fruits, vegetables, and seeds. Without bees, plants would not receive the pollen they need.

One-third of people's food comes from crops that are pollinated by honeybees. Farmers use bees to grow 90 different kinds of crops worth more than $10 billion a year.

Beekeepers also raise bees and sell the honey. Bees produce more than 200 million pounds (90 million kilograms) of honey every year. This honey is worth $150 million.

Beekeepers are worried that killer bees will hurt their honey business. Killer bees might mate with the beekeepers' European bees. This would mean the newborn killer bees would not produce as much honey. Killer bees are also more difficult and dangerous to manage.

Killer bees take pollen from plant to plant.

Learning to Live with Killer Bees

Many people think that killer bees will become the most common bee in North America. But this is not likely to happen. Killer bees do not survive well in cold weather. The cold winters in many areas of the United States and Canada will probably limit their range. Killer bees will be limited to warm southern states and the west coast. Learning more about killer bee behavior is the best way to prevent being attacked. Do not approach or disturb a killer bee hive. Killer bees sting only to protect themselves and their hives.

Wing

Abdomen

Pollen Basket

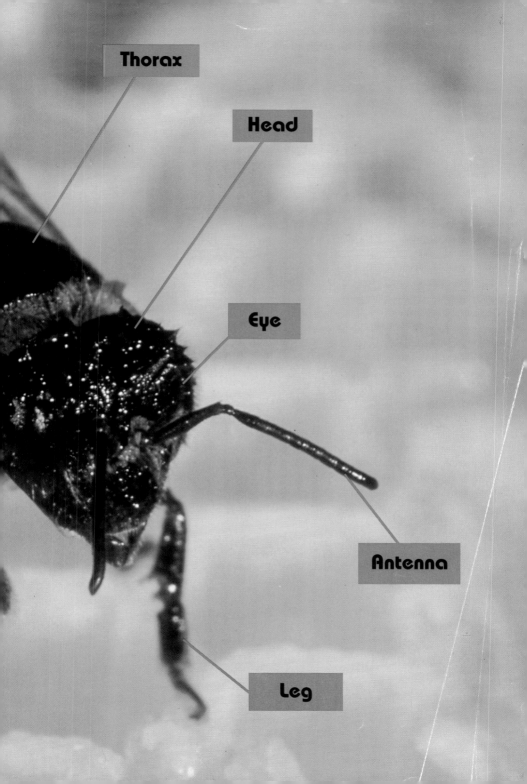

Thorax

Head

Eye

Antenna

Leg

Words to Know

abscond (ab-SKOND)—to suddenly leave one bee colony and find a new location

drone (DROHN)—a male bee that mates with a queen

entomologist (ent-uh-MAHL-uh-jist)—a scientist who studies insects

honeycomb (HUHN-ee-kohm)—a wax structure made by bees that consists of many six-sided cells; used to store nectar, pollen, honey, eggs, and developing bees

nectar (NEK-tur)—a sweet, sugary liquid produced by plants

pheromone (FUR-uh-mone)—a chemical released by bees which causes them to behave in a certain way

pollen (POL-uhn)—a tiny, yellow grain produced by plants

pollinate (pol-uh-NAYT)—to transfer pollen from plant to plant

swarming (SWORM-ing)—when part of a colony leaves to form a new colony

To Learn More

Davis, Kathleen. *Killer Bees*. New York: Dillon Press, 1993.

Lavies, Bianca. *Killer Bees*. New York: Dutton Books, 1994.

Lesinski, Jeanne. *Exotic Invaders: Killer Bees, Fire Ants and Other Alien Species Are Infesting America!* New York: Walker, 1996

Pringle, Laurence P. *Killer Bees*. New York: Morrow Junior Books, 1990.

Useful Addresses

American Beekeeping Federation
P.O. Box 1038
Jesup, GA 31598

The Honey Bee Research Lab
2413 East Highway 83
Weslaco, TX 78596

National Honey Board
390 Lashley Street
Longmont, CO 80501

U.S. Department of Agriculture
Agricultural Research Service
Public Affairs Specialist
Room 448
6303 Ivy Lane
Greenbelt, MD 20770

Internet Sites

Ag News—Africanized Honey Bees
http://agnews.tamu.edu/bees

Africanized Honey Bees Title Page
http://www.intrlink.com/users/stingshield/!AHBTITL
.htm

The Bug Club Home Page
http://www.ex.ac.uk/bugclub

**Roadside America: Killer Bee Capital of the
World**
http://www.roadsideamerica.com/attract/TXHIDbee.
html

Welcome to G.E.A.R.S.
http://198.22.133.109

Index